HELP!

A Daily Walk
with the
Holy Spirit

RECOMMENDED

Helen Rylance

Copyright @2022 by Helen Rylance

This publication contains the opinions and ideas of its author. It is intended to provide helpful and informative material on the subjects addressed in the publication. The author and publisher specifically disclaim all responsibility for any liability, loss or risk, personal or otherwise, which is incurred as a consequence, directly or indirectly, of the use and application of any of the contents of this book.

WORKBOOK PRESS LLC
187 E Warm Springs Rd,
Suite B285, Las Vegas, NV 89119, USA
Website: https://workbookpress.co,/
Hotline: 1-888-818-4856
Email: admin@workbookpress.com

Ordering Information:

Quantity sales. Special discounts are available on quantity purchases by corporations, associations, and others.
For details, contact the publisher at the address above.

Library of Congress Control Number:

ISBN-13:   978-1-958176-50-4 (Paperback Version)
                978-1-958176-51-1 (Digital Version)

REV DATE: 25/05/2022

HELP!

An Everyday Walk with the Holy Spirit

Helen Rylance

Table of Contents

Acknowledgement

I would like to thank Judith who kindly agreed to follow in her late Mothers footsteps, by going through my writings and correcting all my errors. She is as gifted in making my writing legible as her Mother before her. Without her all my faults would be laid bare for all to see.

Well done Judith I am sure your Mother would have been proud of you! I am forever grateful for the time and effort you have put into this book.

Help!

An Every day walk with the Holy Spirit.

By Helen Rylance

My daily walk with the Holy Spirit began in a time of desperate need! My prayer went something like this 'Help Lord! I need a parking place or I am going to be late for work.' Yes! That is really how my relationship with the Holy Spirit works!

I am quite a literal person, I discovered that when as a small child, one day my mother told me to go and throw this. (This being a jug with some liquid in it,) into the pond, we had on our family's land. So I did, however when I returned to the house she asked where the jug was, I told her I had thrown it into the pond as she asked me to. Well, she was not pleased with me, because she had meant that I should throw the contents of the jug in the pond not the jug as well.

As this example of my muddled thinking shows I am clearly in need of the Holy Spirit in my life. How about you?

This Story is about some of my experiences in my fifty plus years of knowing God as my Father, Jesus as my Saviour and the Holy Spirit as my helper. I hope it blesses you as you read it, as it did me in writing it!

Chapter One

I guess like many Christians I felt for many years that the Holy Spirit was something to be scared of......spooky ... the Holy Ghost!

Until I discovered he was a person, a person of the God head. He was there back in the beginning when we were created. When God said "let us make man in our own image!" the Holy Spirit was part of that statement .... us and our image! Right there in the beginning.

As I was born again of the spirit of god I began to be aware of that still small voice, not that I always responded to it, but it was there, inside of me. It was that same spirit that took away my desire to smoke cigarettes and use bad language, on that very first day of being born again.

That still small voice began convicting me of my sin and leading me to live aright...Gods way. Not that I always listened!As I began to read the word of God...the Bible. The Holy Spirit began to lead me into the truth of that word. It was while reading the Bible I began to discover Jesus and the life he led … a pattern laid down for us to follow. It was during this time that I discovered that Jesus was baptised by immersion in the river Jordan by John the Baptist. That still small voice was asking me, 'If Jesus was baptised, didn't I also need to be baptised?' The Spirit of truth, ……... the Holy Spirit kept reminding me that Jesus as sinless man didn't need to be washed clean from sin, but in obedience to his Father he submitted himself to this discipline. So I too should submit myself to the waters of baptism. This I did.

As I continued to read the word of God the Holy Spirit continued to lead me into further truths. Healing I read was something Jesus did for people in his day. "Would he heal me?" I asked. As I prayed and sought God through the Holy Spirit I began to hear that still small voice again!

I had, since I came to know the Lord, been suffering from depression. That seems to be a contradiction in terms. Why did my loving heavenly Father set me free from smoking and using bad language and allow depression to set in? The evil spirits behind the depression had been within me from birth but had not manifest themselves until Jesus saved me. Why? They didn't need to because I was born in my flesh a child of the enemy, when Jesus set my spirit free and I was born again these spirits began to show their power over me by bringing me into the darkness of depression. This I suffered from for three years, using medication to control the effects of the depression. During this time, I studied Gods word and began teaching from it, then I saw in that word that Jesus healed and set people free from evil spirits. "Would he heal me?" I asked, "would he set me free?"

That was when I began to hear that still small voice instructing me as to the steps I was to take. The following week I was due to undergo minor surgery in hospital to have a cyst removed from my shoulder. I clearly heard the instruction as...... "you have to stop taking your medication during surgery, don't take it again when your surgery is over. I will heal you!" That was the instruction .... That is what I did...... The Lord through his Holy Spirit began setting me free from inherited evil spirits.

My mother's family had been involved in witchcraft several hundred years previously to my becoming a Christian. A curse had fallen on her family, as the first Christian in her family the enemy, ... Satan had loosed the demons I inherited at birth into me, but Satan and his demons have to submit to Jesus and to Jesus they had to bow, and leave my body. This was the start of a long healing and deliverance process, and what he has done for me he can do for you!

The work of the Holy Spirit continued in me, gradually as it says in the book of Colossians. 'If you are raised with Christ,' as we are after water baptism we are to desire the things above not on those things of earth or the flesh. The last thing to die is our flesh, our final battle will be with the flesh. Throughout our new life in Christ we will need too crucify the flesh and die to ourselves.

The Holy Spirit will be with us to help and support us throughout this process.

So who is the Holy Spirit and how does he operate in our lives? In John's gospel he is described as the helper, one who comes along side us to help us in our day to day lives. He helps us while we are here on earth, guiding us into all truth. He will teach us all that there is to know about God our Father and Jesus our Saviour .... if we are willing or desirous to learn.

How often does the Holy Spirit bring to our minds a verse of scripture or some teaching we had forgotten? He will confirm God's promises to us, long after we have forgotten.

He has a will, he has emotions, we can grieve him it tells us in the book of Ephesians. His timing is perfect something we come to recognise as we walk with him. He comforts us in our time of need. He is our advocate before the Father, interceding for us, he pleads with the Father on our behalf.

There is no fear with the Holy Spirit for one of his fruits is love and perfect love casts out all fear. In the book of Galatians, it tells of the fruits of the Holy Spirit, all of which are available to us as we allow him to move in our lives, the more of him……. the more fruits we will manifest. He is the one who will convince us of the righteousness we have in God through Jesus Christ which is for all time …eternity. That we are Gods children, part of his family, bearing his likeness.

He is the one who convinces us that Satan is a defeated foe and that he has no power over us.

Another aspect of his character is that he will show us things to come, prophesying is part of his role, it is not man who prophesise but the Holy Spirit through man. He gives us discernment so that we can discern if what is said is by his spirit, or by the flesh, or from the enemy of our souls …. Satan.

We can speak in other tongues using another gift of the Holy Spirit, the gift of tongues another of the nine gifts he brings to us. A gift which all of us can receive, for in the book of Acts chapter nineteen verses one to six it says "Did you receive the Holy Spirit when you believed?" This is not a gift for the chosen few but for us all.

Chapter Two

There is a saying that goes something like 'The apple doesn't fall far from the tree' Meaning we as children are very similar to our parents.

Really!

Then why have I spent the past fifty years or so feeling like an orphan? As a child I was frequently told by my mother's family; 'We were never really sure who your father was.' Not a nice thing to say to a child, is it? Especially as my Mother was married to my Dad!

Even as a Christian, as I followed the path I believed the Lord had shown me I was frequently labelled; Butterfly, Wanderer, Nomad and many other similar comments were laid on me. This often distressed me, but no matter how many times I refuted these labels there was always someone who thought they knew me better than the Lord!

Finally, as I have been writing this book

something amazing has happened! Someone said to me recently. "You're a nomad aren't you, Helen?" My reply. "No I don't think so, usually the Lord leads me." I *don't just wander at will. I thought.*

I can't count how many times the Holy Spirit has said to me as I have questioned the directions given me! "Abraham knew not where he was going, but went." In other words, get moving, stop questioning! That is how my Christian life has been.

Earlier this year one of my brothers told me that his wife had been doing some family research and had found that our great grandfather was a pastor. He had started his ministry in Cheshire and then moved to Durham, England. It wasn't an area that I was familiar with, but decided that maybe I would take a holiday in that area next year and see what I could discover about him and his family.

Then a few weeks ago I met up with another of my brothers and his wife, I told him about this latest bit of information regarding our family tree, knowing he too had started at one point to look into the family history.

As I am the first known Christian amongst my siblings and previous generation he knew I was interested in finding out more about our ancestor Pastor James Rylance. So he began his search to find out more! I was blown away by the information he had discovered, for me it was life enhancing!

As I said earlier, I had begun over the years to enduring much negative comment regarding my life style. I have lived in almost forty houses or flats, worshipped in most denominations and also served in them.

Yes, I had parents that I got on fine with, though they too did not understand my life style. While my Dad died when he was quite young, he was only just turned sixty. My mother was born again in her fifties, and eventually as she became more spiritually alive she began to understand my calling before her death at ninety-five years of age.

Surprise! There in the information very kindly provided by the Salvation Army, was the answer to my calling and wanderings. It was in my gene's!

My great grandparents were James and Evangeline Rylance. I, like them, had started my spiritual journey in the Methodist Church. Then they heard of General Booth who had started the

Salvation Army three years earlier. This they believed was for them. My great grandfather trained as an officer, as did later my great grandmother. He became a Commandant and she a General, as she played her part in the work they were called to do.

They had five children during these early years of service and moved from town to town setting up new citadels for the Salvation Army. One year they were asked to move from Cheshire to Durham with just five days' notice before they were due in post, they made it! Moving from Cheshire they zigzagged up and down the country as well as setting up posts in Scotland, Ireland and Wales.

So much of my gifting began with this amazing couple, they were pioneers, so am I. My calling, like theirs, has taken me from place to place, church to church. Finding my great grandparents has taken away from me the orphan spirit that dogged me for so much of my life. I now know where I came from and who I am. Even my early years were grounded in the Salvation Army as my parents did take me with them on a Sunday to the meeting during the early years of my life.

I can say with confidence that I know who I am

in Christ and who I am genetically. This thrilling discovery has given me a wholeness I have not experienced before in my eighty years on this earth.

Chapter Three

Patience

How many times have you said? "Oh no, not again!" As you made the same mistake yet again, or as the same scripture is given to you through the Holy Spirit?

I used to dread one particular scripture appearing during a time of seeking the Lord for direction. That scripture was 'Be still and know that I am God' my interpretation of that scripture, quite wrongly was 'nothing is going to change!' I would despair of reading those words. After many years I began to realise that those words really meant. 'Wait I am working things out.' Working things out could take a long time and I had yet to learn patience and my faith was very weak. Waiting helps you to increase your patience and your faith will grow, if you don't give up!

We are frequently led by the word of God through the Holy Spirit highlighting certain scriptures.

How lucky was Moses who was given a cloud by day and fire by night to show the Israelites when they should move forward. God had given Moses a system by which he and the people he was leading could understand. That still didn't stop them from getting it wrong by deliberately rebelling, and we are no different. It is only when we come into that relationship with God as Father that we trust him to know what is best for us, this we discover as we grow in our Christian faith and develop patience.

Self-Control

There are many things that can hinder us from growing in our faith and in our relationship with God.

One of these is possessions. Do you really need a new dress or a car or new furniture, curtains, handbags, shoes? The need to satisfy your craving for possessions can be a hindrance to your relationship with God. Buying things can indicate a lack of love for the Lord and a lack of self-control. You are really saying, what you own defines you, but it should be who owns you, that is who has bought you for a price… Jesus, that defines you. Do you hang on to things, long after their time of usefulness? Afraid to be parted from them? This shows our insecurity; in Jesus we have all that we need.

Do you worship at the altar of the family or at the altar of the Lord? We are truly blessed to have families and if we have families who worship Jesus we are doubly blessed. However, does the worship of your family hinder you from worshipping God, of being available to his plans and purposes for you?

Faith

I remember being in church one Sunday, when two men, strangers to the fellowship, came into the sanctuary part way through the service. The pastor invited them to sit down and continued with his sermon. At the end of the service I heard the Holy Spirit say to me "You are having two extra for lunch today".

So I asked my husband if we could invite these two men to lunch, he agreed. So I waited as the pastor spoke to the men and then said, "Is there anyone willing to give these men lunch today?" I said, we would be prepared to take the men home with us. So that is what we did. Scripture tells us 'That we never know when we are entertaining angels unawares'

This was true of these two men who looked less like angels than you could imagine! They had my family in fits of laughter as they regaled them with stories of their experiences. Where the stories true? Who knows! But what a wonderful peace filled our home as we gave hospitality to these men. Since that encounter I have had several encounters with angels, only occasionally have they had wings!

Gentleness

In 2019 I went on a Christian retreat in Oxfordshire with a long term friend of mine. We both wanted to seek the Lord about our future. I had no idea what the Lord would say, if he had anything to say at all, after all I was almost eighty years of age!

During the first evening we met with a group from a local church who had come to pray at the centre. During the time of fellowship that followed, conversation led to my church background. Well, let's be honest, I am considered to be something of a mongrel, having worshipped in many different denominations. I go wherever the Lord leads. "Oh no a butterfly" a man declared in a very derogative tone of voice. The man didn't know me but chose to judge me. Declaring people should not be moving from church to church. "Why" I silently asked?

When the time came for me to share my testimony, I shared something of what the Lord had taken me through during my walk with him over the years. While I was tempted to take a wrong stance with the man who had called me a butterfly, by the grace of God through the Holy Spirit I gently explained how this could only have been possible by moving around churches, churches that taught different elements of the Bible, not all churches teach about the Holy Spirit how he leads and guides us, how we can hear his voice so we can obey his teaching. How can we hear him speaking through the scriptures if we don't know his voice?

When we are in danger how can he alert us if we don't hear his voice? You may think that is highly unlikely in your case but in the world we live in danger is all around us. Does that youth in front of you carry a bomb in his back pack? Will the driver of the car approaching have a heart attack at the wheel? What about the holiday you have booked, flying to your favourite resort or city? Will you know that still small voice telling you not to go there or not to do that thing you were intent on doing?

Do you have a relationship with the Holy Spirit?

Many who believe in Jesus as their saviour do not go on and build a relationship with God the Father, or God the Holy Spirit. They have missed out on so much! Sometimes we have to mix with the right people to come into the blessings the Lord has for us.

As a young Christian I was introduced to a missionary, who in turn brought me into the circle of the Baptist missionary society. I loved reading books about missionaries and their escapades. Reading in the book of the Acts of the Apostles I realised that I too could have similar adventures with my heavenly Father. Faith seemed to be the key to most of these people's lives I read about. When I discovered that without faith it was impossible to please God I was even keener to study the saints of old. Abraham, it says in the bible, 'He knew not where he was going but he went!' He left his home and his family and along with his nephew set off on his journey, where to, he didn't know, even then he followed the Lord through the Holy Spirit. In the first book of the bible, Genesis, it tells us that Jesus and the Holy Spirit were there in the beginning of creation with God. Abraham was led by God.

Did he make mistakes, yes of course he did! He was human, he told lies, and twice he said his wife was his sister to get himself out of trouble. When God told him that he and his wife Sarah would have a son, he decided to do it his way, considering his wife to be too old to bear a child. So he slept with Hagar his wife's maid and she conceived Ishmael, what a mistake that was! We are still paying the price today through the activities of the Arab world.

Finally, after God sent some angels disguised as men to tell him that in the following year, Sarah would bear him the long promised son, the one he had spoken about through his Holy Spirit all those years before. He laughed, falling to the ground in his laughter, as did Sarah as she sat in her tent, eaves dropping! How could she a ninety-year-old woman conceive a child, even assuming that ninety-nine-year-old Abraham was still up to the job!? But with God nothing is impossible to those who believe, and Abraham still believed.

Just as the Lord had said Sarah conceived and bore Isaac their son. When Isaac was a young boy God challenged Abraham to go to the land of Mariah where he was to offer his much loved son as a sacrifice. So Abraham set off to the place God through his Holy Spirit had told him to go. God spoke to him! Abraham obeyed even though he knew that he was being asked to kill his own son. He had even brought the wood and fire needed for the sacrifice.

When Isaac asked Abraham where the animal for the sacrifice was, he told his son God would provide, such was Abraham's faith in the Lord, he believed that God would not let Isaac die at that time. When God has made you a promise be ready to be tested as to how much value you place on your relationship with God over your value of what has been promised. As we know, God did provide a ram for the sacrifice, but not before Abraham had bound and tied his son and placed him on the altar. As he raised the knife to kill him, an angel spoke and told him not to continue with the sacrifice, there caught in the bushes by its horns was a ram. Just as Abraham had predicted the Lord had provided.

If Abraham had not had a relationship with God, he could not be sure that he had heard his voice. It is said Jesus learned obedience by his death on the cross, Abraham was learning obedience by his relationship with his heavenly Father.

We all need the Holy Spirit we need to hear his voice and respond positively to that voice whenever we hear him, I say Him because he is a person in his own right as the third part of the God head.

Getting to know the Holy Spirit may save your life one day. When I lived in Israel, a friend of mine was travelling into the city of Jerusalem on the bus one day, she was on the way to the dentist but she got held up in a traffic jam. Realising she was going to be late she became angry. She knew this would entail financial penalties which she could not afford as she was already late for her appointment. As she spoke to her saviour, peace entered her soul, she knew God was in control. Finally, she arrived on the street where the dentist was situated, only to find she could not enter as there had been a bomb blast just outside the dentist. Several people were killed and injured, if she had been in time for her appointment she could have been one of them, but God through his Holy Spirit delayed her.

Chapter Four

So who is the Holy Spirit? As Jesus prepared to leave his disciples he promised them a comforter, one who would lead them into all truth. He told them he would ask the Father to give them a guide, a comforter one who would lead them into all truth and would be with them always.

This Holy Spirit was not going to be available to those people of the world. He is only available to those who love Jesus and keep his commandments. This he repeated. When the Lord repeats something twice we need to pay attention, this is important He told them that he would live within them and be with them always, if they loved him and kept his commandments.

Jesus went on to say, "He who loves me will be loved by my Father And I will love him and reveal myself to him." When asked why he would reveal himself to them but not to the world,

He answered. "I have told you these things while I am with you. But the Father will send the Holy Spirit in my name, he will teach you everything and remind you of all that I have told you. He will be a helper…. He will bring to mind all that the Lord has said to you." Do you forget? he doesn't, ask and he will remind you. He will lead you into all truth, no one else can do that, but if you lean on him he will lead you into all truth.

In the first book in this series '**So you think you've messed up**' I share with the readers the way the Holy Spirit led me as I read in his word the truths of the power he has placed within each one of us who believe. Some of these I am going to share with you in this book. I questioned him as to whether this power still existed and if it did how could I receive those blessings associated with that power that lies within each of us who believe. The Holy Spirits power will be different in the way it operates through each one of us but it is still the same spirit. You may be a hand I maybe a foot but we each have a role to play as the Holy Spirit is manifest in the body of Christ through us. So we each receive God the father, Jesus his son and the power of the Holy Spirit. All three are within, but do we have a relationship with each of them?

Peace

A gift we all receive when we receive Jesus as our Saviour and Lord is the Holy Spirit in the form of peace. One of the first experiences we have as we receive Jesus as our Saviour, is peace. I still remember the peace I received more than fifty years ago, a peace that passes all understanding and keeps our hearts and mind in him, if we don't have that peace something is wrong! The living word is not in us.

Jesus said, "If a man loves me, my father will love him and we will come to him, and make our home with him. However, he who does not love me does not keep my word, because the word you hear is not mine but the fathers who sent me."

"Peace I leave with you; my peace I give to you"

Peace is a sign that God has everything under control, trust him! Do you have that peace? Do you really trust him to take control of your life? So many people even Christians, are unwilling or even afraid to relinquish the control of their lives to one who loves them and died for them. Even worse they seek to control other people's lives.

Peace can be a sign that all is well, while the absence of peace may be the Holy Spirit trying to point out there is a problem. Do you have that peace?

Word of knowledge

The Holy Spirit gives us direction or words of knowledge. When I was writing the first book in this series the Holy Spirit spoke clearly about putting a key on the front cover. *Why? I wondered,* but did it anyway. I looked for a suitable key and arranged with the publisher to place it in a prominent place on the front cover. Several years later I met a lady who told me the story of how she was led to read. 'So you think you've messed up.' The first book in this series.

She was about to come out of prison, where she had come to know Jesus as her Saviour. A lady who helped her get settled into her new life gave her a word of knowledge. ...A spiritual gift her helper was blessed with. She told her she would find a book with a key on the front cover. The Lord through his Holy Spirit would use the contents of the book to bless her, and it did. She had a problem, she didn't have money to spare to spend on books. While visiting a nearby town she felt prompted to go into a second hand book shop. Looking along the shelves she found it, she was so excited, it was just as the Holy Spirit had told her. It set her free to serve the Lord, which she has been doing ever since. Today she has almost finished her university degree and is serving the Lord wherever she goes.

When the Holy Spirit prompts us we have a choice, ignore it, believing we have misunderstood, or we can run with it. How did I know the key was what God required me to do? It was the peace I received that convinced me! It was peace that enabled this dear one to pursue finding a book she could ill afford to buy.

Chapter Five

What about the hope the Holy Spirit brings us? In the book of Romans chapter fifteen it talks about 'The God of hope filling you with all joy and peace as you trust in him, so that you may over flow with hope by the power of the Holy Spirit.' So often in my life this joy of the Holy Spirit has filled me with such joy despite the difficulty in my life. One such occasion was noticed by a then work colleague and friend, Alma. She telephoned me one New Year's Eve to ask if I was going to visit my friends who lived in her area. I told her I was. She asked me to call in on her before I visited them, it was important! She emphasised.

Later that evening I called to see her. It was then that she told me that during our working together despite the problems in my life I always seemed joyful, and it showed on my face! She wanted what I had got!

After a life time of being a committed catholic

she still did not have any peace or joy despite the fact she went to church every day!

I talked to her about Jesus, how he had come into my life, bringing me peace and joy through the Holy Spirit as I invited him to become my Saviour and Lord. "Could she have that joy and peace" she had asked. So that very night she asked Jesus to forgive her of her sins and come and be her Saviour. What a privilege and joy to be able to see another soul won to the Lord.

Sometime later, we took a trip to Israel and the scales began to fall from her eyes as we visited various sites related to Jesus. We would study the scriptures after our day touring the land. Finally, on our last day we visited the river Jordan. My Pastor, who had organised the tour, asked if anyone wanted to be baptised in the river whilst we were there. Alma accepted his offer, and I was blessed to be part of that ceremony of seeing her make another step in her spiritual journey.

The joy of the Lord is our strength. Why do we so often feel weak, cast down in our spirit?

In our daily lives if we do not walk with the Lord through his Holy Spirit we will feel weak, it is he who gives us the strength to live the life he has planned and purposed for us. However, if we are not walking according to his plan, expect to feel weakened, for that often means we are walking in disobedience - sin.

Joy is a fruit of the Holy Spirit.

Standing on his promises

Standing on the promises of Christ our Saviour gives us hope. How can we have hope that our children will come to see Jesus as their Saviour, when with our eyes we see them living in inappropriate ways. Stand on the word of God by the power of his Holy Spirit. His word says 'You and your house hold will be saved.' God has promised, he does not lie or change his mind. Your children may have left home, they are still your children and his promise never changes. So don't let the enemy rob you of your joy and peace because your children are not living as you would like them to live. Keep praying. Don't give up, I don't pretend that it will happen immediately but the Lord does hear and will fulfill his promise. Because hope does not disappoint us when we are in Christ Jesus...

Healing

What about his promise to heal? We are told in

scripture that we are healed by his stripes. The stripes he received when he was beaten before he was crucified. The beating he took on our behalf. With that shed blood we can be healed, if we receive that healing, believe and it will be yours.

However, some years ago I needed a hip replacing, I was in agony with the pain. I prayed and prayed, believing Jesus would heal me through his Holy Spirit. My hip wasn't healed, but I had peace. God was working it out. Finally, I got an appointment to go into hospital for the operation. This was when I realised he was going to use a doctor to heal me, not the miraculous gift of healing. Did hope die, no! God was still in control. This was just as well as I woke up in the middle of the operation to hear the nice young doctor swearing!

Later he told me, as he apologised, that he had not known that I had osteoporosis. When he took hold of my hip bone it just melted in his hand, he freaked out, and did something he did not usually do - swear!

The fact that I came too during the operation was not neglect as we knew I had a problem with anaesthetic and finding a right balance between over dosing me and giving me too little is a fine line, this time it was too little. In past it has been too much, and then the doctors struggle to get me round again after the operation! But thankfully God is still in control. Within six weeks I was driving my car and have been able to encourage others to go ahead with their operations.

Praise and Tongues

The Holy Spirit has many gifts to give us; these are intended for the benefit of the body of Christ. Again I found this out through reading the Bible; again I wasn't in a church denomination that believed in the gifts still being operational today. I always took the view that as Jesus was the same yesterday, today and forever the gifts he had to offer us through his Holy Spirit were still the same and still available.

When I sought the Holy Spirit about praying in tongues, I was surprised to hear him say 'I have given you the ability to praise me in your own language.' That was true, ever since I had been baptised I had been able to praise Him in English. Was this evidence of having received the power of the Holy Spirit when I was baptised? I could praise him for long periods of time. So why did I want another tongue to praise him in? I kept asking. 'Why do you need this?' he asked. I told him that as I had become involved in the healing ministry I needed a language that Satan could not understand. Finally, I began to speak in another language. So often we want to speak in tongues for self-gratification, even showing off! I needed it to set captives free from the enemy, so I was granted my request. So how does that work? I can prayer in my tongue to communicate with God through his Holy Spirit when I am unable to know how to pray in given situations. This gives us a direct line to God, then the correct answer to a problem becomes clear, it may come to my mind or through the Bible or through someone else. This type of praying is done quietly or silently not out loud.

There are other tongues that can be spoken aloud in a fellowship. This type of tongue needs an interpretation; you may have been given that gift as well, though often it is someone else who will interpret. The use of this tongue is usually a message for someone in the fellowship or even a visitor to demonstrate the power of God. It is advisable not to use this tongue unless you are sure there is someone available to interpret.

We can be surprised how differing tongues can speak to people. I remember a tongue being given in what was clearly an oriental language; a visitor was delighted to receive this message from God as she had been seeking God for some time about an issue, and she had had to visit this fellowship in order to get the answer she needed. I wonder sometimes if God wants to test our obedience, so calls us to visit another fellowship to get the answer.

Interpretation of tongues

Another of the Holy Spirit's gifts is the interpretation of tongues. If someone gives a message in tongues will you be brave enough to give the interpretation, even if you have not done so before? You will know you have the answer by the way the words form in your mind.

So there are various gifts, but the same Spirit. There are different ministries, but the same Lord. There are various activities, but it is the same God who operates all of them in all people. But the manifestation of the spirit is given for the common good. So if you have received a word of wisdom, a word of knowledge, the gift of faith, gifts of healing, or you are able to work miracles, prophecy, discern different spirits, use various tongues or interpret a tongue, these are not to bring you glory, but to meet the needs of the body of Christ through the power of the Holy Spirit working in us.

I was happy when I received the gift of tongues, because it meant I had another tool in my tool box of equipment to serve the Lord. We need to collect tools for ministry, they help to save souls, bring peace to others and often inner healing.

Discerning of spirits

How can we be sure if what we are hearing is from the Holy Spirit? In the first book of Corinthians chapter fourteen Paul says "With men of other tongues and other lips I will speak to this people; but even then they will not hear Me"

Another gift of the Holy Spirit is the discerning of different spirits. This can be used to identify if it is the Holy Spirit, and also can be used to distinguish between various spirits.

In the book of James, he talks about how we need Wisdom from above …. The Holy Spirit is wisdom.

James says "Who is wise and understanding among you? By his good conduct let him show his works in the meekness of wisdom. But if you have bitter jealousy and selfish ambition in your hearts, do not boast and be false to the truth, this is not the wisdom that comes from above, but is earthly, unspiritual, demonic. For where jealousy and selfish ambition exist, there will be disorder and every vile practice.

Submit yourself to God and the enemy will flee from you," Finally, submit every thought and imagination that is not of God to him and he will make straight your path.

Chapter Six

Words of knowledge

I have often been to a Christian centre in the centre of England, and have experienced many blessings through attending these meetings.

One of the things that I have frequently had to get over, is how many people forget my name. In one day I can be called several different names by people I have known for years. I have to laugh many times over these errors. One day I just laughed and said "Lord no one ever remembers my name" The following week I went to a conference for four days.

On the first night one of the speakers was giving 'words of knowledge' by pointing to people and saying, "You in the pink shirt, or you in the green jumper" etc. Suddenly the same man called out my name "Helen" I didn't move because Helen is quite a common name in England. Once again he called my name. This time

I stood up. He called me to go forward to the platform. Where he told me that the Lord knew my name it was written on the palm of His hand. During the following days this man continued to point to people and call them out by the garments they were wearing. On the final night, two ladies who had been sat in front of me throughout the conference, turned to me and said "Do you know you are the only person that has been called out by name?" God was making a point; one he makes to each one of us who are called his children. Your name is written on the palm of His hand. He knows your name!

Hearing his voice for you is so very important. Yes, we can be given a word by someone else, and that can be exciting but there is nothing like hearing from God in person. The word of God say's 'He calls his own sheep by name, and he leads them out. The sheep follow him because they know his voice.' Also, 'for eye has not seen or ear did not hear nor has it entered the heart of man the things which God has prepared for those who love Him' When God said in the book of Jeremiah I know the plans and purposes I have for you.' I certainly could not have imagined the many ways God would use me when I was much younger.

Another word of knowledge given to me was

when I was the leader of the local Women's Aglow. When the guest speaker arrived he entered the meeting room giving out words of knowledge from the Lord. I was busy booking people in and carrying out administration tasks, so I didn't get included in this distribution of gifts. Later in the evening when everyone had gone home and we were about to say our final good byes to our speaker, he stopped and said to me "You have been badly abused verbally all your life by your mother. You have to tell her to stop doing it!" My reply to that was "As she is in a care home and can barely speak let alone hear I think that it is unlikely that I will get an opportunity to do that!" I thanked him and we left the building to go home. While I had very little faith that I would get the chance to talk with my mother as during my more recent visits she had not spoken a word and was confined to her chair.

The next day I visited my mother and was shocked to see her standing with her walking frame at the door waiting for me! She greeted me with a warm smile and then started talking to me! She suggested we went up to her room where we could talk without being disturbed. We got into the lift and she carried on talking. I was both pleased and surprised to see what the Lord was doing.

We entered her room and as we sat down she continued talking about what a handful I had been as a small child. I then told her about the visiting preacher we had had at the Women's Aglow meeting the previous evening and how he said I was to tell her to stop speaking in negative ways against me. Her reply was typical. "Yes but like I just said you were quite a handful when you were young." Did that justify decrying me to anyone who would listen now that I was in my seventies? I had been blessed with the ability to forgive my mother almost immediately the deed was done, but it was something she still needed to learn. It was such a blessing to have that conversation with my mother because forever afterwards she went back to her non-communicative ways. It seemed like the Holy Spirit had touched my mother that day for that one purpose, for me to let her know that she was forgiven.

I find it interesting that the Lord knows just where we are hurting and at the right time he deals with it.

You can hear Gods voice and still ignore Him. Jonah was one such person, he was called to go to Nineveh. He knew God wanted to save the people of that city. Jonah wasn't happy about that; he didn't think these people deserved to be saved.

To avoid the call, Jonah got on a ship going in the opposite direction. We need to learn a lesson from Jonah because we can find ourselves in real danger if we decide to disobey God. Jonah finds himself caught up in one almighty storm. It was so bad that the crew of the ship began throwing the cargo overboard. When the captain of the vessel found Jonah in the hold of the ship sleeping instead of praying, he was not amused! The sailors had drawn lots to find out who was to blame for this dire storm they found themselves in. The lot fell on Jonah, they questioned him and discovered he was running away from God. Then Jonah knowing these people had been dragged into a mess of his making, so it was then he told them to throw him into the sea. As they tossed Jonah into the sea the tumult ceased.

However, God had known that Jonah would be unwilling to fulfil the plan he had for Jonah to preach to the people of Nineveh, so he had prepared a big fish. This fish would swallow Jonah and after three days it would spit him out onto dry ground. After three days in the stomach of a big fish you would have thought Jonah would have held his hands up in surrender to God! But he didn't he had to be taught another lesson before he was willing to cooperate with God.

Are we like Jonah? Of course, we go through

many more difficulties than we need too, because like Jonah we have our reasons for not wanting certain people to be saved, our bias, our prejudice of certain people groups causes us to drag our feet when God calls us to help with the harvesting of souls.

Writing has become part of my way of winning souls to Christ. These books have been totally written under the influence of the spirit. I just used to sit at my computer and let the spirit lead me, there were no plans, story outlines or thoughts of what was coming next. Which is probably evident from the seven books themselves! Many is the time I have sat at my computer laughing hilariously as the story unfolded taking a route I could not have envisaged! Through the power of the Holy Spirits conviction as readers have searched the pages of my books many have come to know Jesus as Saviour.

A series of books that I wrote called 20-20 Vision have been a blessing to others in another form. One day I felt the Holy Spirit leading me to write a musical based on the thought of not being saved and then being left behind after Jesus has come and taken his own home to glory.

Again I wrote the musical based on the story. The scenario went something like this, children were in the classroom, when whoosh they all disappeared! Buses, trains, aeroplanes, and all kinds of vehicles were crashing out of control as their Christian drivers were all taken home to heaven. Leaving carnage on the streets of the world. As parents went to collect their children from school many were shaking their heads in bewilderment as they were met by shocked school teachers, staring at the empty seats in their classrooms. Parents asking "What's happened? where have the children gone?"

Some of the people of the fellowship in the village where I lived joined together to put on the production. We found songs and hymns that fitted the theme and slotted them into the appropriate places.... having first asked for permission to use the music. A great many people from the village and surrounding area came to watch the production. The Lord through his Holy Spirit was thinking outside of the box to proclaim the gospel yet again.

If we live in the spirit, let us also walk in the spirit.

Chapter Seven

It is the Holy Spirit that calls you to positions of service to his people, your brothers and sisters in Christ. Sadly, the church of today rarely recognises those God has called, rather choosing men in their own image, their own friends or family members. After all, choosing someone who may challenge their thinking, or potentially undermine their position is too threatening to contemplate for some.

Not many churches recognise the role of an apostle any more, despite the word of God stating that God has put these in the assembly, first apostles, second prophets, third teachers after that those who perform miracles then those who are gifted in healing. Then those who help in any way, those who govern and finally those who speak in tongues. In the book of Ephesians, it also includes evangelists, all these roles are for the equipping of God's people for the work of service needed in the building up of the body of Christ. A body that I truly love, whilst recognizing that not all who say Lord, Lord will be saved.

In my fifty plus years in the church I have held several leadership positions, until I became a divorced woman, despite the fact I was the innocent party, I was still asked to step down by church leaders. The leadership positions identified in the New Testament of the Bible are elders or overseers and deacons. What is the qualification for these two roles?

Clear guidance is given in scripture, and these should be people who are; blameless, the husband of one wife, sober, self-controlled, respectable, hospitable, able to teach, not given to drunkenness, not violent, not greedy for money, but patient, not argumentative, not covetous and one who manages his own household well, having his children in submission with all reverence. Wow! that is a tall order, but as the word goes on to say, if you can't manage your own household how can you possibly take care of the assembly of God?

He must not be a recent convert, lest pride becomes his downfall as the devil seeks to trip him up. Moreover, he has to have a good reputation with outsiders. Very few people fall into this category, today we have women elders, gay couples in leadership and many new converts to say nothing of those who have never received Jesus as their Lord and Saviour.

What of deacons? They are to be honorable, not insincere, not given to drinking too much wine, not greedy, keeping the mystery of the faith in a pure conscience. They are first to be tested, when they are found blameless, they can then serve as deacons. They must be the husbands of one wife, manage their homes and their children well. Likewise, their women folk must be honorable, not slanderers, sober and faithful in all things.

Baptism

There is a baptism for believers, not many churches teach about this, certainly the Baptist church does and several others.

I first read about this baptism in the bible. I read that Jesus came to John the Baptist and asked to be baptised. John was not that keen to do this, even though he knew that there was one coming whose sandals he was not fit to untie. When Jesus presented himself to John to be baptised John saw the spirit of a dove descend from heaven onto Jesus and remained there. John said in the word "He who sent me to immerse with water said to me, the one on whom you see the Spirit descending and remaining on, this is he who immerses with the Holy Spirit. I have seen and borne witness that he is the Son of God."

When I had seen in the scriptures that Jesus had been baptised even though he was sinless, I too wanted to be baptised. However how was I to accomplish this when I belonged to a denomination that did not believe in this baptism? When I prayed about it, I was led to the local Baptist church where they were teaching about what Jesus said on the subject, after all he was sinless yet he was baptised by immersion. We need to show people what our faith is about; dying to self as in baptism, is a good starting point.

John the Baptist said that Jesus baptises with the Holy Spirit. When, how? I soon discovered that there were fruits of the Holy Spirit Once again I am seeking the Lord about what I saw in his word.

Fruit of the Spirit

I believe that one of the most important functions of the Holy Spirit is to develop within us fruits of his spirit.

I remember as a young Christian coming across a poem that talked about the way the Lord develops the fruit of the Holy Spirit in us. It was not encouraging! But none the less as the years have gone by I have discovered it is true.

The verses of the poem stated that if you desired to have the fruit of love, you would find yourself in situations where you found it difficult to love someone! If you were seeking to receive the gift of joy, you may find yourself in a situation where you had to praise God in all circumstances, even through the hardest of times. The fruits of the Holy Spirit cannot be produced by the flesh, so the flesh has to be crucified in order to release the fruit of the Holy Spirit. The verses of the poem drew a picture; the picture was one where whatever you sought you would be placed in a situation that was the reverse of that particular fruit of the Spirit. We often seek the peace of God only to find our lives becoming out of control. What is God playing at? He is not playing games with us, the truth is the grape can only produce the wine according to its type, likewise the production of the fruits of the Holy Spirit can only be produced by being in difficult situations.

Look at what Paul had to say to the Galatians.

First of all, he points out what are our fleshly fruits, none of which are to be sort after. These are; adultery, sexual immorality, impurity, lewdness, idolatry, sorcery, hatred, strife, jealousy, rage, selfishness, dissensions, heresies, envy, murders, drunkenness, carousing and the like! Do you look at this list and think; well this doesn't apply to me. Really! We all go through a phase where we become selfish or self-centered, that's the flesh, this will not die until we leave the earth and take up our residency in heaven. However, we can speed its demise by crucifying the flesh on a continual basis.

A month after I came back from my final visit to Israel I had a mini stroke. It was New Year weekend; the doctors were all shut. I had no telephone to ring my family even if my brain had been functioning in that way. I didn't know my neighbours as I had only just moved into my flat. I still don't know how long I sat in my flat, but eventually as I prayed I felt I should go outside and walk. Walk! I staggered down the corridor and out of the front door, bouncing off the walls as I staggered along. On the street I fell into the gutter like a drunk! Several times each day I did this. Two weeks later I was able to visit a doctor, who tried to get me to walk in a straight line, but failed miserably. Many months later I was diagnosed as having T2 strokes these I was told I had suffered from since I was ten years old. These T2 outbreaks have manifest in different ways; from being paralysed for three months at the age of ten years old, to having M.E in my fifties. This has left me with hands that tremble terribly and often worries people. But it doesn't affect me except when I am typing on the computer, when it takes twice as long as anyone else because the trembling finger on the keys produces more letters than is necessary!

The thing that shocked me most was in my head the only words I had were swear words. Nothing else! Strangely despite my loss of speech I knew in my spirit that the ability to swear had been taken away from me when Jesus saved me. So why was the thing that offends me so much in the forefront of my mind? I puzzled for months as my speech returned and the swear words disappeared once again. "Why Lord?" I asked over and over again. Finally, one Sunday a visiting preacher explained!

The last thing to die in us is the flesh, was what he said. Eureka! That was the answer. For months I had sought the Lord and now here was the answer I had been looking for, actually if I had searched the Bible I may have found the answer sooner, because Paul talks about this in his book to the Romans, but I didn't I just prayed!

These works of the flesh need to die and be replaced by the Fruits of the Holy Spirit. Really what we need to do is kill them off by replacing them with the fruit of the spirit, and yet how can we do that?

If we look at the fruits of the spirit, we can see that every one of them is demonstrated in Jesus life. Love, joy, peace, patience, gentleness, goodness, faith, meekness, and self-control. These nine fruits are visible in his life. Even when he over turned the tables in the temple, he did not lose control. When he was hanging from the cross and the thief next to him started talking to him, he didn't tell him to "Shut up" like we might have done. No! He showed him love. In meekness he submitted to his Father in being willing to die in our place, taking the punishment we deserved, as he cried out in the Garden of Gethsemane. "If it be possible take this cup from me!"

We cannot achieve the fruits of the spirit all in one day or year. I believe it will take us a life time. We demonstrate many of the fruits on occasions, but they will be fleeting, as we need to learn to die to self.

The more we do this the more of the fruits of the spirit we will gain. However, without pain there is no gain. Jesus learned through suffering, therefore so will we!

Those who are the Lords, the word says "Have crucified the flesh with its passions and lusts. If we live in the Spirit, let us walk in the Spirit." We wonder why painful situations come into our lives, many unsought. We are being conformed to the image of Jesus. As the saying goes, you can't make wine without squeezing the grapes!

Love

Love, Paul says is the greatest gift of all. Without it we are bankrupt. Why do we love God? because he first loved us! David said in one of his Psalms, 'I love him because he hears my voice.' Why do you love him?

John in one of his letters reminds us 'This is love; that we walk according to his commandments' He meant the ten commandments laid down in the Old Testament. When Jesus was asked what is love? He told us to love one another as he has loved the world and to love your neighbour as yourself!

Love ourselves, is he kidding! Look at what we do to our bodies, cover them in drawings known as tattoos, we cut our bodies, because we are not satisfied with the way God created us. We abuse our bodies by eating and drinking too much, we are overweight, even obese, is that loving ourselves. In my ministry to those who are damaged, hating themselves is often what motivates them in their thinking. Teaching them to love themselves as Christ loved the church, his body, is a privilege and I am blessed by it.

During the Covid pandemic many Christians have been showing their love for their fellow man by helping with food banks, distributing food and clothes to those in need. One such group in my hometown have received much publicity for their good works. This particular group gave all their energies to providing for those in need, not only the usual items but meals and electric meter cards and prayer. Many have come to know Jesus through this demonstration of love.

I remember as a child that food was in short supply. One Christmas we had left on our door step a box of groceries, what a blessing and a demonstration of God's love, that I personally remember to this day.

We who have received such blessings, I believe, have a greater responsibility to demonstrate our love in similar ways. So we are called to walk in love as Jesus did who gave himself for us as a fragrant offering and a sacrifice to God.

Chapter Eight

The armour of God

How do we stand against the enemy of our souls when he seeks to attack us? We must put on the whole armour of God so that we can stand against the schemes of the enemy. While I believe that when I put on the armour of God it is on at all times except when I sin. If I have put on the girdle of truth and then fall into lies and deception, I have exposed that part of my body.

If I have put on my breast place of righteousness and then fall into sin by not living as a child of God should. I can expect an arrow through my heart sent by the enemy because I am not living as God intended I should, and my breast plate of righteousness has become ineffective.

If I choose not to share the gospel with someone when I have the opportunity, I can expect to feel like I am walking without shoes on as my feet may no longer be fitted with the armour of protection to my feet.

Walking without the shield of faith in our Lord Jesus leaves us unable to wield the shield of faith which will give us total protection from the fiery darts of the enemy.

When we are saved from our sin we wear a helmet of salvation, which protects us from spiritual death. Finally, we need the word of truth in our hand for the word of God will kill off the enemies lies. We have to store the truth of the word in our hearts, memorising Gods word enables us to use that word against Satan when he comes against us.

So put on the whole armour of God, the shoes of the gospel, the girdle of truth, the breast plate of righteousness, the helmet of salvation, taking up the shield of faith and the sword of the spirit which is the word of God every day to be sure you are covered at all time.

Thoughts

Take captive every thought and every imagination that exalts itself against Christ Jesus. What does this mean?

One of the ways that Satan tries to rob us of our peace is through our minds…. thoughts of all kinds can rob us of our peace. We need to store in our memory a verse of scripture, particularly one that relates to any area we are easily got at by the enemy.

Not feeling God's love? Try what the Lord himself says. "I will uphold you with my right hand"

If you can't remember scripture at that moment of attack, remember to take captive every thought and imagination that raises itself against Christ Jesus. For no temptation has overtaken you that is not common to man. God is faithful and will not allow us to be tempted above what we can endure, but will make a way of escape, that we may be able to bear it.

God has a purpose behind every trial or tribulation that comes into our lives. Psalm 34 states. 'The Lord is close to the broken hearted and rescues those who are crushed in spirit.' 'I will never leave you or forsake you' he says to us in our time of difficulty, and that is true. So often when I feel abandoned in times of difficulty I am reminded that God is not a liar, and as he promises he will never leave us, we can depend on that truth.

Now that my hair is grey I am reminded of his

promise that 'even when your hair is grey He will be with us.'

We learn things through suffering that we could never learn any other way. We draw closer to God as we call out to him. We see more of his love manifest in our lives. When the going gets tough I think of some of these people.

Joseph is my favourite go to character. He was put in a well by his brothers, then they sold him as a slave, but God was in control, He made sure Joseph was allocated a safe place where he was used to God's glory, it was only when the lady of the house took a shine to him that things got difficult again. He ended up in prison, but even there he was used by God to help others. Finally, he is released, after having a bath and a shave he is called into Pharaoh's presence. He made himself clean before he entered the presence of the ruler of Egypt, as we should before we enter the presence of our Lord and Saviour.

Pharaoh and his officials listened to what was said about Joseph's talents and they began to think that he was a man who could help them through the coming difficulties they were about to experience as a famine was set to hit the nation.

What we do and how we react in the dark times, can help prepare us for future use in God's kingdom. Nothing is wasted, every experience we have had can be used to bless someone else. I have found that almost all my life, my experiences can help someone else.

Just yesterday I was speaking with someone whose ex-partner had died. He was clearly shocked despite the lady having fulfilled her three score years and ten, he was shocked at his own grief. I was able to share with him my own experience when my first husband died. My son telephoned me to say that his dad had died after a long illness. I had to put the phone down as I burst into tears. I went through a long grieving process and felt like a widow. This was thirty years after the divorce, why this happens I am not sure but I believe after a divorce we don't necessarily lose the love we had for that person. I remember my dad saying that he loved my mum right up to the end of his life, and while they were divorced and remarried to other people, he still he felt that way.

Chapter Nine

I have always enjoyed being married, it isn't about status though I have enjoyed that too, but the companionship and being able to work together is a blessing. When you know God has called you to a marriage relationship then how can it go so badly wrong? Some may argue that it wasn't Gods will in the first place. When you have God's word to confirm that calling you feel sure it will work well, but that is not always true. Mainly because some people stop walking with God. Consequently, even in Christian marriages where jealousy and envy sneak in, it becomes difficult to change the atmosphere over the relationship. When one of the couple's eyes start wandering, the pain sets in. The pain of rejection and disappointment begin and can start to erode love, but even this can be overcome by God's grace. This testimony reinforces this truth.

There was a point in time when I met someone I would have liked to marry. The man had been separated from his wife for more than three years when we met. The elders of his fellowship had agreed that the marriage was over, but that they should separate for three years before they divorced. We met and fell in love as this three-year period was coming to an end. We agreed that we would seek the Lord about marrying once his divorce had gone through. So we separated and gave ourselves to seeking the Lord.

The interesting thing was that the Lord said the same thing to us both. He was to return to his wife and seek reconciliation. I heard the Lord clearly say that we would not be meeting again that he was sending him back to his wife and family. I was heartbroken, but accepted that was the Lords will. That marriage was restored and renewed. God can do it, but then why did he not do it for me when my marriage broke down?

It was late August when the Lord laid it on my heart to go to the Bank holiday weekend conference. I had gone to this annual Christian conference that was held in a local university, in previous years. I was with my friend Alma. My husband had not wanted to attend this particular year but had said he did not mind if I went with my friend. So after I had finished my shift as a receptionist at a Christian centre, we left to attend the afternoon session.

I had heard the speaker, Erwin Rutherford, an American, before, he was a good speaker and I was interested to hear him again. The conference was held annually and always had a theme, during the afternoon session the speaker preached on the chosen theme. After he had concluded, my friend and I went and had a meal at a nearby restaurant, after eating we returned for the evening session.

When the speaker stood up to speak that evening the first thing he did was apologise to the conference leaders, he explained that during the interval, as he prayed over the message he had intended to bring, the Holy Spirit had spoken to him and told him to speak on a different subject, that of Destiny!

At this point my companion became excited and dug me in the ribs with her elbow and whispered, "This is for you!" Certainly my ears pricked up because recently the Lord had been speaking to me about my destiny. As usual I had not got a clue about what he meant! But I was about to get it spelt out for me!

After a preamble about what it meant to have a destiny, something we all have, that is why we were put on this earth. In the book of Jeremiah, we are told "I know the plans and purposes I have for you, plans to bless you and do you good" Says the Lord? What the speaker said next did not constitute my idea of a plan to bless me. He said that as he had prayed that afternoon he had heard the Holy Spirit say clearly that there was someone present who should leave their partner!

How could that be true, I had already had two husbands, surely the Lord would not issue such an instruction, after all didn't he say "I hate divorce" And of course he does say that in his word the bible. Why then? I was shocked, but I knew that was what I had to do.

Alma and I talked about what the speaker had said after the meeting had finished, we had talked in the past of my husband's attitude towards me, his wandering eyes and how he had taken to verbally cursing me... Let the reader understand he did this in a biblical fashion, meant to harm and damage a person. It was an inherited family thing, something his dad had done, with great effect, destroying many a person, but his dad was not a Christian; however, my husband professed to be one. I had begun to refute the curses, thus nullifying them, but was this any way to live as an active, committed Christian? I had begun to wonder. I had spoken to him about the cursing but to no effect, at this point we had been married for ten years.

A few days later I told him what the Lord had

said through the speaker at the conference, having prayed about this word, there was no argument about my going, I was just told to go! What I didn't know was that the month prior to the conference, George had transferred our savings from our joint account to an account in his name! I was not aware of this but God was and knew the motive behind this action.

Shame

Despite the fact that I believed the Lord was in the ending of this marriage, shame still dogged me! There were Christians who said to me God hates divorce and I believe he does. He says so in his word. Coping with the shame was not easy, the enemy of our souls taunts us, taunted me. The Lord teaches us to stand against the enemy by quoting scripture at him. This is what Jesus did when he had been sent by his father to the wilderness. Here Satan tempted him in a variety of ways, each time Jesus quoted scripture at him and Satan left him.

Frequently over the following years I would have to quote scripture to the enemy to get him off my back. It seems to me that when people, even Christian's have something against us the enemy attaches himself to that anger, bitterness or resentment arrowed at us. This results in fiery darts coming at us, which can rob us of our peace if we don't have on the armour of God.

When Jesus died upon the cross he took upon himself all our guilt and shame. If we confess our sin he is faithful and just and will forgive us all our sin. Thank you Jesus for taking away the shame Satan would seek to lay on us.

Chapter Ten

Homeless

I was sixty-seven years of age and about to become homeless. I felt impressed upon me to leave and only take the bare essentials with me. Where would I go? As usual the Lord had a plan in place. A member of the fellowship we belonged to was leaving to visit New Zealand for a few weeks and needed someone to care for her cats, so it was agreed that I would move into her house while she was away. Taking a single bed, two chairs which belonged to my sister and a bedside cabinet, a couple of towels and some cutlery and a plate, dish, cup and saucer and a pan, I left and did my house sitting thing!

A few weeks later I saw an advertisement in a shop window in the village where my daughter was living, it said someone was wanted to house sit while a couple went on a five-month trip to Australia. I applied for the position, and was accepted. The property was directly opposite my daughter's home!

As my house sitting job was nearing its end, two friends in my fellowship began praying for something more permanent. It was then that I was offered another house in the same village it was owned by one of the church members and her sister; it had been their late mother's home. I was looking for a long term home and they had agreed that I should have a long term contract. However, the owner had left a lot of her possessions in the house and would frequently come in while I was out and rummage around. I was paying council tax on the property but she would increasingly add to her pile of possessions. Then there was the added stress of frequently being given notice to quit when the sisters had a disagreement.

By this time, I had developed a problem with my hip, it became necessary to have my grandson live with me, as I reached a stage where I could only walk by holding onto the furniture. When a bungalow became available in the village I got a lease on that property, and my grandson moved in with me, he then lived with me until he went to university. Now I was waiting for an operation to have my hip replaced.

On the move

Just as I received a date to have the operation I also received an offer of a flat that had been newly built. I was on the move again the fourth time in three years. My daughter and sister moved my possessions to the new flat while I was in hospital.

Having my hip replaced was an interesting experience; it was a private hospital, a lovely place. The doctor was a pleasant young man and everything about the place was great, however I don't have a good track record with anaesthetic. Knowing the difficulty previous doctors had had reviving me after an operation, they decided to give me less rather than the normal dose. What they didn't bank on was giving me too little. The result! I woke up in the middle of the operation to hear that pleasant young doctor swearing! They quickly put me under again. When the doctor visited me later he was very apologetic. He explained that they had not known that I had osteoporosis. When he took hold of my hip, it just melted in his hand. He said he was so shocked, the bad language just popped out of his mouth, he was mortified, poor man!

Soon I was moving around on my crutches and a week later I was home, having moved into my new flat. Within six weeks I was driving my car. I had frequently prayed the Lord would grant me a gift of divine healing but that was not what he wanted for me. My recovery and freedom from pain has encouraged several people as they too have undertaken this surgery and were fearful of the outcome. I was able to encourage them by telling them how worthwhile the operation was, free from pain, able to walk again. Go for it I say!

Chapter Eleven

Godly not a God

God wants us to take on his values, attitudes and character. In an effort to bring some of these values into my life God moved me into a flat, it had no garden and I love gardening, but it did overlook a field.

The flat was one of six; the building was three storeys high, two flats on each floor. It was an experimental build; they had several innovative systems built in. It was also experimental in the choice of its occupancy. The first floor had a very young couple and a lesbian couple with a baby.

On the second floor was myself a seventy-year-old pensioner. A young couple with a young son. On the top floor was a single mother with her teenage daughter. Above my flat was a single young man, who had a games consul that he would dance too.

We regularly had visits from the police. Sometimes it was the young man on the ground floor, who happened to be a drug dealer! His clients would ring the doorbell or bang on the window to wake him to buy drugs in the middle of the night, and he frequently escaped through the down stairs window when running from the police.

The lesbian couple frequently had fights, again the police were involved, and finally they split up and divorced. Not before they had sought my help on several occasions to assist with the injuries inflicted when one had head butted the other and they needed to use my telephone. Wonderfully, eventually one of the women gave her life to the Lord.

The teenage girl enjoyed smoking cigarettes outside on the steps of the building with her friends, laughing and singing in the early hours of the morning. Then there was the young man who loved his games consul with its dance programme, not much peace from the constant dancing, when they built this experimental building they didn't think about such things!

On the move again

Finally, after three years a friend offered me a

lovely bungalow in the area I still live in. Again sadly that only lasted for three years, when the owner who had been in a care home died and the property had to be sold. Once again I was homeless, at seventy-five I had to dispose of all my possessions, I just had two suitcases full of possessions that I left with my youngest son as I set off for Israel again, alone.

Israel

When we married, we had both been in previous relationships. I had been married twice, these relationships I speak of in the first book in this series 'So you think you've messed up' George had been married once and also had lived with a long term partner. Our pastor had declared us to be equally experienced in life and was satisfied that this was of the Lord. However, I have since wondered if that is really a good basis for marriage, we really needed counselling before our marriage, but then hindsight is a wonderful thing.

Ten days after our wedding George had a breakdown and was at home for ten months. Was this due to an earlier comment he had made when he said he had asked the Lord for a wife like Helen, but not Helen! I have wondered since if this was what was behind his behaviour during our marriage, was he still looking for someone else?

Our pastor was into the healing and deliverance ministry. He and his wife were quite experienced at this type of ministry and had been involved in it for many years. They worked tirelessly with George for many months and finally declared him to be a new man, as they had dealt with his pain and past hurts. He was changed. Sadly, some years later he declared that he did not believe in their ministry and that there had been nothing to be set free from. The pig had returned to its vomit as the scriptures say. When we deny the Lords touch on our life we allow back into our lives all the evil the Lord has cast out and often more beside. This is what George had done, but the evidence of this denial would only be revealed later.

A year after our marriage God called us to Israel, I had been involved with an organisation in Jerusalem for some years and I noticed in their news magazine that they were looking for a cook to make lunch each working day for their staff. We talked it over and decided I should apply and offer George's services as a handyman, and we were accepted. It was hard work but very enjoyable as we worked with some lovely people who encouraged us in our work.

It was during this time that the Lord began to

speak about the vision he had given me many years before I met George. The vision was about a house and a ministry of serving others. I knew the house had five bedrooms and numerous bathrooms, but where it was I had no idea. While working in Israel we took on a rented property in the heart of the city on the edge of the Old City of Jerusalem. It was during our stay there that our landlady asked us if we knew anyone who wanted to rent a large house in the Jewish Quarter of the Old City. Were we interested in it? She asked. We were just about to go back to England for a holiday, so we promised to let her know our thoughts on our return in a month's time. It was during this time that someone in our fellowship gave us a word of knowledge from the Lord. We were about to be offered a large house in a key location, the speaker gestured with her hands indicating a road junction.

The House

We returned to Israel and spoke to our landlady to request a viewing of this property. She had previously mentioned that the state of the property was indescribable; so much structural damage had been done by the five children of the family living there. It was unclean to put it mildly. Despite all that we felt the Lord wanted us to take it.

The property was in a key location, at the junction with the Arab Quarter of the Old City, and had been built five hundred years previously for the grave digger on the Mount of Olives the Jewish burial ground.

Some years later I had a surprise encounter with the man who was the head of that family. I was accompanying a friend who was on a mission to give money to a Jewish organisation. She had arranged to meet the man at a local hotel on the Mount of Olives. When we arrived at the meeting point the man glared at me and I wondered why, he looked vaguely familiar but I didn't know why. As my friend commented later, he doesn't like you I wonder why; did I know him she asked? We had to meet him again later, it was then he revealed who he was and our connection.

He was an American Jew. He and his wife had produced five boys in little over five years, and his wife who we met was heavily pregnant with their sixth child, a girl. He told me how the strain of having so many children had caused his wife to go into depression, consequently looking after the house and the children had become too much for her and he had to try and earn enough money by working and then help in the house when he came home. They had got into debt with their rent and despite help from their fellow Jews they were unable to manage. Consequently, the landlady had given them notice to leave. At that time, we knew nothing of this. All we knew was God was calling us to take on this shambles of a house, with its thirteen damaged doors, holes in the wall and more than forty steps from the front door, up to the lounge.

This was the house of my vision, but it did not look a bit like the exterior of the house that I had seen in the vision but it had all the bedrooms and bathrooms. We had been blessed with friends who had the skills to repair the building. The landlady was thrilled to allow us to use it as a bed and breakfast, something she had long wanted to do, but was far too busy to put it into action.

It was several months before the family moved out and the property was repaired. We left our employment and started looking for furniture to furnish the house. Soon people came from all over the world to stay; we never advertised the property it was all done by word of mouth. Several months later we noticed an elderly rabbi saying prayers over our house and we discovered from friends who knew more about the local culture that he wasn't wishing us well! He was cursing our marriage along with anyone else who stayed in the property.

Debris

One day we heard noises in the street, it went on for a few hours but we didn't think much of it. Until

I looked down the stair well and could see that something was covering the window in the door, we decided to go down and investigate. Looking out we saw that the whole of the street was covered in debris, large cardboard boxes, food and general detritus. We lived next door to the rubbish room and someone had pulled all the neighbours rubbish out and put it on our steps and in the street in the front of our house. As we started to move the mess back to where it belonged, two young religious Jews came round the corner and when they saw the mess asked what had happened. They said that they knew who was responsible and would report them to the local rabbi.

Once the mess was cleared and we had thanked our ministering angels, we found ourselves with another problem. We couldn't get the key in the lock, our local protagonists had carried out another of their favourite tricks, and they had put glue in the keyhole. Fortunately, one of our guests was leaving that night and he was sleeping in the only room in the front of the house. With a little pebble throwing and a lot of shouting we managed to wake him up to let us into the house.

Prior to this incident we had on several occasions found piles of wood on the door step. On several other occasions boxes. It meant nothing to us but according to Jewish culture it meant Get out!

Here is some wood to make some boxes for your possessions and leave!

The bed and breakfast had been operating nearly year but was not yet covering the enormous rent we were paying. The price of property in Israel is exorbitant. Before we took the property on George had said if it didn't make a profit in the first year, we would have to go home. While I was used to living by faith and would have trusted the Lord to provide, George wasn't at that stage yet and I felt I should support him with what he felt comfortable with. We started to pray the Lord would send someone to take over and he did! A young American couple took over until they were conned out of it by an older American lady who promised them she would bring some of her followers in to look after it. However, she didn't she closed it down. They were gutted, but the Lord knew that in their hearts they wanted to serve him, sadly both our marriages broke down. The rabbi cursing had had its effect!

Why did the Lord not protect our marriages? After all, both couples were serving the Lord. Who knows, perhaps we had been complacent and not protected our marriages, though in my case I had already seen my husband's wandering ways with our guests.A confirmation, as if I needed one, that God sees all. After all he does say in his word the

"That whosoever looks on a woman with lust in his heart is guilty of adultery!" We all need to strive to adopt Jobs attitude which was "I made a covenant with my eyes not to look with lust upon a young woman" or in a woman's case, a man. Sadly, in the church with our close relationships it is all too easy to cross the line

Chapter Twelve

God's purpose

Rick Warren in his book The Purpose Driven Life says God longs for you to discover the life he created you to live - here on earth, and forever in eternity. In the book of Romans, it speaks of God knowing what he was doing from the very beginning. He decided from the outset to shape the lives of those who love him along the same lines as the life of his son. The Son stands first in the line of humanity he restored. We see the original shape of our lives there in him. In the book of Jeremiah, he says 'I know the plans and purposes I have for you, plans for good not for evil.' So why do we feel we so often miss the mark?

We are being changed into the image of Jesus; this can only happen by facing the challenges in life by the power of the Holy Spirit to overcome those difficulties. We cannot do that through our own strength, our flesh. Trusting God, the Holy Spirit to lead and guide us is the only way. If we are to become like Jesus we need to change.

So were did Jesus start? By being obedient to his parents! Where did he end, by being obedient by his death on the cross?

After he had been to Jerusalem for the Feast of Passover, a time when the Jews who could afford it went up to Jerusalem where the feast was celebrated each year. Whole families and communities would travel together, most walking all the way. It would take Jesus family at least three days to walk from Nazareth. It would have been there in Jerusalem that Jesus would celebrate his bar mitzvah. As we know from scripture he was approaching thirteen years of age at that time, this was the age that this public reading of the scriptures in the synagogue took place.

On the journey home Mary and Joseph lost sight of Jesus and eventually had to backtrack to find him. When questioned by his parents about the fact that he had not stayed with the group, but had spent time with the Rabbis studying the Torah, the Jewish word of God, they rebuked him. It was then that he replied that they should have known that now he had completed his bar mitzvah he would want to be about his father… God's, business. It is almost as though his parents had forgotten that he was the son of God. However, Jesus did not argue with his parents, rather the word tells us that he returned home with his parents and was obedient to them. This is an interesting response by Jesus because according to Jewish tradition, once a child has gone through their bar mitzvah they can legally make their own decisions about life, though it is expected that they will discuss any major decisions with their parents, though officially the choice is the child's now, as they are now considered to be responsible for their own lives .... An adult. However, Jesus chose to be obedient. 'Although he was a son, he learned obedience from what he suffered and, once made perfect, he became the source of eternal salvation for all who obey him.' This as children of God should be our response to God our father, obedience.

Another lesson we can learn from Jesus. At this young age, when his parents found him he was discussing the scriptures, with those more learned than himself. Always be willing to learn more from the scriptures, even though Jesus was the Son of God he was willing to humble himself and learn from others.

Jesus carried out practical, physical hard work. He didn't sit around and expect to be provided for by others, he learned carpentry from

Joseph, he worked in the family business until he was thirty years of age. He did not rush into ministry, thinking I am the Son of God. It's time to get out there and show the world who I am! No, he waited for the right time, his heavenly father's time. Then what did he do? He started to lay down a pattern for us.

He had heard that John the Baptist had started his ministry; he knew of John; they were cousins though seemingly had never met. When Jesus turned up at the site on the River Jordan where John was baptising people, he requested that John baptise him, John refused at first, this was not only family, this was the Lamb of God who was destined to take away the sin of the world! Why should he a mere man baptise the Son of God, a sinless man? One whose shoe laces he was not fit to untie.

Jesus set us the example of being baptised by immersion, even though he had gone through all the Jewish rituals, and was sinless having kept the law, still he was baptised by immersion. This was another act of obedience. Therefore, we who are sinful should also be baptised even if we were baptised as babies. Baptism is also an act of witness, showing the world that we have become one of Gods children. Interestingly it says in scripture that it was then that the Holy Spirit descended onto Jesus, he was also baptised into the Holy Spirit. This is another reason we too should be baptised as we receive another empowering of the Spirit.

Jesus ministry started immediately after this anointing for that is what this imparting of the Holy Spirit was. The following day some of John's disciples left him to follow Jesus.

When I was baptised by immersion, the water was very cold as the heater meant to heat the water had broken. Some denominations do not believe in what is often known as adult baptism, I was in one of those churches at the time, the leaders did not believe in baptism and my friend and I were ostracised by the leaders for a time after undergoing baptism. We stood our ground and quietly pointed out what the scriptures said about it. We were blessed to see each one of those who opposed us, baptised themselves within a year. It was costly to be obedient, we were ostracised, but even more costly for the minister of the church he lost his job because he was willing to be obedient. Then he and many more of us left the denomination and set up and independent fellowship, which God blessed and used.

I have been blessed by sitting at the feet of many excellent teachers. One man I had met was teaching about waiting on the Lord. He himself had been an Intercessor and had been used mightily by the Lord in the Second World War, interceding for Britain. However, his teaching did not sit well with some of his colleagues who were not trained intercessors, his teaching was not where they were at spiritually. He was ostracised and he and those of us who followed his teaching were called heretics. For him it was seen as a great shame, a slur on his character. Ten years later these same people retracted their condemnation and apologised saying that they too had come into the same teaching. Following your teacher can cost you, anyone who follows Jesus must expect to pay the price as there are Pharisees who bad mouthed Jesus and if you mean business with Jesus they will persecute you also. If we go through the hard times with him, then we are certainly going to go through the good times with him!

Sadly, many people become bitter rather than grow in the grace of God and fail to grow up. We must respond in the same way that Jesus would.

That is what happened when my marriage broke down, and as a result I suffered the loss of several friends because of the half-truths they were told by my ex-husband, they must have been glad to take on board the fake news and as a consequence lose my friendship. A problem of many insecure people is that they feel they must put other people down in order to raise themselves up. We are called to love them anyway, just as Jesus did. Love those who hate you and do good to those who despise you.

We are being conformed to the image of Jesus, he is seeking to change us into his image by the power of the Holy Spirit, this is often through suffering, and how we respond to suffering can shape our character.

Chapter Thirteen

Botanical Gardens

Because I would visit Israel several times a year, I always had to seek the Lord as to where he wanted me to be or who I should be meeting with. Each visit brought different connections. At one point I was led to the newspaper column that was advertisements for volunteers. It was here that I came across a lady looking for help in the Botanical Gardens. She needed helpers to keep the British section of the gardens in good order. English speakers required, Wow! Just what I needed.

I love gardening and I only knew a few Hebrew words, so conversation was impossible. When I met the lady in charge I discovered she was an English Jew from the London area. I was taken on to help with the back breaking job of weeding the garden. Sunday was the day that we carried out this work. It was great, I loved it. I met several people who I became friendly with, though standing around talking was not permitted but you could talk and work at the same time!

After I had been there several years I was told I was to be given a special assignment the following week. I was so excited. I prayed all week about what I was going to be doing the following Sunday. Sunday of course for the Christian is the day of rest and going into his house for worship, but in Israel Christians mainly meet on a Saturday, though the King of Kings fellowship meet on Sunday evening, which is where I enjoyed going.

Finally, I arrived at the gardens for my appointed task. I was asked to clear a particular patch of ground, where I was to plant some seeds known in Britain as Honesty. As I worked the ground the Holy Spirit spoke to me. Clearing the weeds from the ground was like praying out the enemy of our souls from people's lives. If we want to see people come to know Jesus we must first clear the ground to allow the seed of the word of God to be sown and take root. If the ground is not ready the seed won't germinate and take root. Then as the ground is watered, so the ground that the seed of the word has been sown into, in a person's life has to be watered in prayer. The Holy Spirit told me it wasn't enough to pray blanket prayers over people but to pray for them by name. What a thrill it was when I returned for my next visit to the land of Israel to see the seeds I had sown, blooming. This was a promise of a future harvest of souls about to be brought into the kingdom of God.

Prayer was part of my mandate for being in Israel. Frequently people would stop me in the park or on the bus and start talking to me; finally, they would get around to asking me if I was a Christian. I often wondered how they knew, I didn't wear a cross or carry a bible, as it was inadvisable to attract attention to myself. Evangelising in Israel is illegal, but if someone approaches you and asks about Jesus that is acceptable. On one occasion on a bus trip to a village where John the Baptist was born I had three separate encounters with Jews seeking Jesus. One was with an English mother and her daughter, who had converted to Judaism, when they heard English speakers sat behind them they turned to talk to us. Then on the same bus an American student also got into conversation with me. I ended up taking him around the village we were visiting sharing with him the gospel as we walked. Later on the return journey we were led to share Jesus by someone else who approached us. How did they know we were Christians?

Finally, a taxi driver solved the query, while sitting in his cab as he drove us to our destination one evening; he asked if we were Christians. I asked how he knew, he replied that Christians in Israel carry an aura about them; he could see that aura, as could those seeking Jesus. Ah mystery solved! So if you find yourself in Israel and you get approached by a stranger, they know who you are if they are seeking Jesus.

One day the Lord said to me through his Holy Spirit, I want you to start praying for people by name, so at that point I started collecting a list of names, working in the gardens was a useful way of collecting names. Occasionally Batsheva who ran the British section of the Botanical gardens would invite me to the Shabbat meal on Friday night. It was lovely to meet local Jews many of them Rabbis, but I was always a bit wary of what I said. My experiences with religious Jews when I lived in the old city had caused me to be nervous of those who didn't speak to me first. During the meal there was always a quiz. One particular night Richard, Batsheva's husband had organised the quiz.

The difficulty was that I knew most of the answers to the biblical questions, but the rabbis didn't. At first I felt too embarrassed to speak, but when no one answered I whispered the answer to the lady sitting next to me. She just told me to tell them

The question was, what the name of the Promised Land was, answer Canaan. Which just goes to show that though they read their scriptures anywhere and everywhere they are not taking much in, but then isn't that true of us also? When I think I have been reading the bible every day for more than fifty years I am saddened by how little I really know. Sadly, the older I get the less I am retaining. However, thankfully I know who my Saviour is and he is my redeemer and long may it be so!

As one of my visits to Israel was coming to an end I had packed my suitcase and on leaving it at the hotel where it was to be picked up from, I was informed that I had to be at check in at three in the morning, they wanted to do a special check on my luggage! The last taxi to the airport was leaving at midnight, so I had to wait in the airport for several hours.

There were no chairs to sit on, so I sat on one of the tables that were used for putting the suitcase's contents on. Sitting, swinging my legs, I prayed. I had perfect peace. It became obvious from the line of single passengers that was developing that the airport authorities were having a splurge on checking the contents of single passenger's possessions. Rightly so! Israel has its fair share of drug smugglers, and innocents like me can soon be sucked in without the Holy Spirit to guide us. This particular night I had nothing to fear and my belongings were soon checked and passed as safe…. but that was not always so!

Staying in Christian Guest houses you don't expect to find the baddies there, but the enemy of our souls is cute, what better place to hide than in a respectable house!

For single travellers, particularly women you feel safer and have more companionship in Christian guest houses. The one I used in Jerusalem was run by a lovely American Christian couple. I got to know them quite well in my early years of visiting the land because I would often pay three visits a year, so as long as this guest house was open I stayed there. Many years later, when they had retired and we were running our guest house they would stay with us. Our roles were reversed.

On one occasion I became friendly with an Irishman who was touring around the middle eastern countries. He had a series of guide books that he had been using on his travels. During one conversation he told me his mother lived in London and that he planned to visit her on his way home. He had decided to send the books by parcel post to his mother and collect them from her at a later date. His thinking was, it would save him carrying the books he didn't need any longer.

When he found out how much it was going to cost him to post the books, he told me he would just have to carry them in his luggage as the price had been exorbitant to post them. As I was leaving the following day I suggested that I take them to England with me and post them from there to his mother. Am I stupid or what? The Irishman went off to Samaria for a few days and it was time for me to go home.

That night I could not sleep, I had no peace. Eventually I prayed. It was then that the Holy Spirit said the books could contain drugs. Really I thought! He went on to explain that this was a well-known method of transporting drugs. At first I thought I was imagining all this, I could not perceive that this was at all possible. Still I had no peace and my lack of peace increased. Eventually I took the books out of my suitcase and left them in my room. The next morning, I told the man who was running the guest house what I had done and asked him to inform my fellow traveller when he returned.

When I arrived back in England I told my daughter and her husband what I had done, she went ballistic! "Mother are you stupid? those books probably had drugs sprayed on the pages, Don't ever offer to do anything like that again, you may not be so lucky next time!"

Thanks to the Holy Spirit I was saved from what could have been a possible prison sentence. Listen to that still small voice!

Chapter Fourteen

2016 was the year of my final visit to Israel. It was the year I turned seventy-six and became homeless yet again. It was also the year my mother died, at the age of ninety-five. She had been living in a care home for about four years, mainly because she could no longer walk unaided and though she shared her home with one of my brothers, he became unable to look after her. We had been told that dementia had set in, however I refused to accept that prognosis as no one in my family had ever suffered from this debilitating illness.

So I prayed. "Lord I refuse to allow my mother to be labelled as having dementia, I don't know Lord what she is suffering from but I don't believe it is what the doctors have said." For a year I prayed in this vain. One day my mother had a fall at the home and banged her head, so they took her to the hospital for an x ray. It was through this X-ray that they found she had a benign tumour on her brain, not dementia as had previously been thought. The Lord heard and responded revealing the truth.

It is my belief that when these wrong diagnoses are proclaimed over a person, a spirit carrying that disease attaches itself to the person and causes them to become ill with what has been spoken over them. Fear can also cause us to open ourselves up to illness when it is spoken over us.

When my mother died, she was no longer in contact with most of my siblings. Just one of my younger brothers and myself did meet with her right up until the end. The other siblings and some of their children did come to the funeral which was lovely to see. However, there was never anyone to grieve with me or mourn her passing.

It was only as I met up with some of my Jewish friends in Israel that I was blessed with someone to talk to about my mother and her life. I had met Ted a Canadian Jew at the Botanical gardens in Jerusalem. He had introduced me to his wife Elaine, they had kindly invited me to their home and showed me round the village they lived in on the edge of Jerusalem, near the border with Bethlehem.

We had walked the same tracks as the prophets

of old, that was so exciting. It was Ted and Elaine who recognised that I needed to be able to talk about my mother and sat Shiva with me. (This is what Jews do when someone dies.) They took me out for a meal, they took me walking and we sat and talked about my mother. What a blessing that was to be able to talk and feel the release of grief that I had carried for months and years. So as my siblings showed no interest in their mother in her old age or after her death, I was blessed by these two dear friends who held my hand and comforted me as I grieved.

It was during that trip that I was out with Riva, my former landlady. Having met up to have an ice cream in a Jerusalem ice cream parlour. I had stayed in Riva's apartment many times in the past, but during a previous trip Riva had told me she was selling her apartment. She worked very hard keeping the apartments in beautiful condition, but as she was approaching sixty her husband thought it was time to sell the properties as they were a lot of work for her.

We had arranged to meet up to catch up on each other's lives and enjoy an ice cream at the same time. It was during this time of sharing that I saw the door close, literally before my very eyes. As I saw this closed door I knew it was the door closing on my work of over twenty years in Israel. I shared this experience with Riva and she asked what I would do, where was I going to live, for she knew I was homeless and also that I had no household items or furniture. Riva and I had a common faith. While she was a Jew and I was a Christian, we both believed in the same heavenly Father and his provision for us. It was one of the things that bound us together. I told her I believed the Lord would provide a home for me and all that I needed. Though even I was surprised at how quickly he did that!

I had been in Jerusalem six weeks and it had been a very fruitful six weeks. Sharing the truth about Jesus with several Jews on several different occasions. Now as I said good bye to Riva I told her that I would now wait upon the Lord to see how he led me.

Half an hour after I left Riva I received a text from a man who I had met earlier in the year who had several apartments in the area I hoped to live in. He was offering me an apartment that he thought would suit my needs, it would be available on December 1st, the very day I would arrive back in England. I said YES! It proved to be just the right one for me.

My eldest son was picking me up from the airport on my arrival at thirty minutes past midnight.

midnight. I was to sleep at his house that night, and then my sister would come and pick me up and take me to do the shopping I needed later that morning. We planned to visit the town I would be living in to buy the furniture. However, my son suggested I go to a large town nearer his home, his thinking was I might be able to get most of what I needed there and anything I could not get there I might find in my home town. The idea being that if I went to the nearest store it would save us having to double back on ourselves if they didn't have what I needed. Good thinking son!

I had bought all I needed in less than an hour, had I gone the way I intended I would have missed some lovely bargains. It sometimes pays to listen to your kids! I met up with the landlord and signed the contract at mid-day. I was home! I just had to wait for the furniture to be delivered, so I slept on the floor for a couple of nights, but that was fine, no hardship there. Once again the Lord had provided me with a home and all that I had need of.

What happened next came as a complete surprise. I had been back in England almost one month, it was the end of the year and a new one was about to begin. It was then that I became ill, really ill. I had no phone, I didn't know anyone, and I didn't know what to do! To this day I don't know what happened, I felt ill, but what is ill? I just sat most of the time, but what was most worrying was my mind seemed to be empty; all I had was swear words running around in my head. It was so frightening, because all I could think was. "Lord you took away my ability to use bad language when I came to Jesus, why is my head now filled with words I don't want to use?" I was scared. "Had I lost my salvation?" I remember thinking.

I could barely walk and my hands were stiff and almost useless, and I was hallucinating what should I do? It was then that I heard that still small voice "Go out and walk" So I went out, literally staggering down the street, falling into the gutter! It was a good thing it was New Year, if anyone noticed they probably thought I had, had too much to drink! I couldn't walk for long, but I kept going out for short walks. Eventually my mind became clearer. I didn't see a doctor for how long? I still don't know, but eventually I did get to the doctors, they didn't know what had happened. They had me walking down the corridor at the surgery, unsure why my balance was so bad. A lovely young doctor couldn't sort it out, so she sought the help of a more senior doctor, he didn't know what was happening either. They said they would send me for a scan, it took five months for the appointment to come through by which time I was quite well, though my left hand was still not as strong as it had been. The appointment was in a town more than thirty miles away. However, a kind friend took me in her car because, while I was driving I could not drive for long distances. Which was just as well as the scan left me unbalanced once again?

A month later I got the results, I had, had a stroke! It was called a T2 stroke. The consultant explained that throughout my life from the age of ten I had manifested this illness in various forms.

It started when I was ten. I woke up one Sunday morning to find myself paralysed, and I remained that way for three months, then it took another three months to learn to walk again and I was in a lot of pain. This problem continued for more than ten years. Until I grew out of it, or so it seemed.

A few months after my second marriage broke down, I developed M.E. This time I had to give up the very good job that I had. Within two days two different Christians told me that the Lord had told them to speak to me and tell me that if I didn't give up working I would not come into his plans and purposes for me. So I retired and spent twenty hours a day sleeping, until God called me to speak to the people of Northern Ireland about the situation in that land. It was during that time, that as a team we only got four hours sleep a night and twenty hours travelling and ministering.

We prayed and wept with many people throughout Northern Ireland, and the Lord brought peace to them, and healed their broken hearts. On the final day we were in a town where tragically several people had been killed in an IRA bomb attack. It was there as we had been ministering in a church for several hours to damaged, hurting people, that a very angry man burst into the building. During our time in this church we had prayed with many people, though none as angry as this poor father whose daughter had been murdered. As he wept and grieved for his beautiful daughter, an only child. We wept with him, finally healing flowed into him, this poor man found peace through Jesus. It was while I was in this healing atmosphere that I too received healing from my M.E.

My life of sleeping twenty hours a day was over, I was out of work I had lost my home, but the Lord had it all in hand.

Chapter Fifteen

Becoming friends of God

Becoming friends with God is encouraged in the scriptures but how often do we hear this preached? The Lord began to speak to me about developing my relationship with my heavenly Father. The word says. 'Anyone who is joined to Christ is a new being; the old is gone, the new has come. All this is done by God, who through Christ changed us from enemies into his friends.' Do you have a friendship with God the Father?

'Now we can rejoice in our wonderful new relationship with God. All because of what our Lord Jesus Christ has done for us in making us friends of God.' Making us friends? Do you really feel as though you have a friendship with your heavenly Father? I didn't. When the Holy Spirit challenged me about my lack of this relationship I thought how could that be possible?

I started to get alongside my Father in heaven, even cuddling up to him in the spirit. Talking to him, singing to him, feeling his warmth. Sharing everything with him, not holding back. Sharing my pain and heartache even my victories. Of course he knew all about these anyway but part of relationship is sharing what is important to us. There are things in our Christian life that we can't share with our earthly friends, they can seem silly to others but nothing is too small to share with a loving Father. For those of us who have lacked an earthly father it is healing to be able to share with our heavenly Father in this way.

Jesus said, "I no longer call you servants, because a servant does not know his master's business. Instead I have called you friends, for everything that I learned from my Father I have made known to you."

We are called to be sons of God, his children. In a normal family set up, parents communicate with their children about forth coming events, in as far as they relate to their children.

From a study of God's word, we can learn of future developments. Even non-believers are beginning to see that life on earth is coming to a close. The frantic efforts of people seeking to stop the so called climate change will not stop God's plan to bring to a close the earth in its present form. Providing a new heaven and an earth where we who know him will receive a new body, and will receive a new home. Surprisingly we will also be working in heaven! The Lord shares his plans with us, personal plans and plans for all mankind. The Lord says. "If any want to boast, they should boast that they know and understand me, because my love is constant, and I do what is just and right. These are the things that please me. I, the Lord, have spoken." Draw close to God and he will grow close to you.

God said to Job's friends. "You haven't been honest with me or about me as Job has." A key to friendship with God is being honest with him, tell it as it is! He won't beat you up for it, rather the reverse; he will love you for it!

Moses was another who said it as it was to God, in his frustration with the Israelites he declared. "Look, you tell me 'Lead these people' but you don't let me know whom you're going to send with me... if I'm so special to you, let me in on your plans .... Don't forget, this is your people, your responsibility.... If your presence doesn't take the lead here, call this trip off right now! How else will I know that you're with me in this, with me and your people? Are you travelling with us or not?" ...... God said to Moses," All right, just as you say; this also I will do, for I know you well and you are special to me." WOW can you imagine talking to God like that? Do you talk to your friends like that? I rest my case! Pour out your complaints before God and tell him all your troubles, just as the Psalmist encouraged us to do.

May your prayer be; 'the thing I seek most of all is the privilege of meditating in God's house, living in his presence every day of my life, and delighting in his incomparable perfections and glory.'

On another occasion I heard the Holy Spirit speaking to me about a place called Blacko. Blacko, where was that? Assuming it was a place, I had never heard of it. I prayed for some time and then began to hear the leaders of the fellowship I belonged to speaking of this place.

I decided to speak to them about my perceived calling from God to this place. It was then that I found out that the leaders had been asking the Lord to send someone to this village called Blacko. I shared with them what I had wondered was a calling from the Lord to go to this place, though where it was I had no idea!

The leaders prayed and later confirmed to me that they believed the Lord through his Holy Spirit was indeed calling me to spy out the land in this village. So as a fellowship they laid hands on me and sent me out. The village was about ten miles from where I lived, so I set about trying to find out more about the village and what was going on there.

There was a church there, but it was closing down I discovered on my one and only visit to it. I discovered that a couple who had been part of this fellowship lived in the village, I say village it was two rows of houses on each side of two roads, and a school and of course a church building, which the denomination that owned it were in the process of selling. Geoff and Lynn felt of the Lord to hold a meeting in their home for anyone who still wanted to meet as a group of believers, so I joined them.

The church building was bought by a local millionaire builder, rumours were rife as to what he would do with it. Sadly, this man was not thought of kindly even though he believed in God and had experienced a meeting with Jesus he did not believe in the Holy Spirit.

Rumour had it that he was going to change the building into flats, not uncommon in this part of the world.

After meeting in the home of Geoff and Lynn for several months it became known that the owner of the building was going to open it once again as a church, and the owner was going to pastor it, a brave move for someone who had never preached or held office in the church. At that point I felt I should move to worshiping in this new venture. What to expect I didn't know!

I use the word brave to describe this man, because anyone who sets up a church, and doesn't know the Holy Spirit and has never preached had to be brave or foolish, take your pick, you decide!

That first week there was no music, his wife eventually agreed to join him and played the keyboard, but the first week she wasn't there. The hymn books were some very old ones with hymns I had mostly not heard of. That brave man got up and preached, his sermon lasted all of five minutes and it could best be described as taking a drink of warm water. It quickly became evident that the poor man was not familiar with the New Testament and what Jesus came to do. The few people who had attended the opening soon left and only his family members he had coerced into coming and myself were left.

What was lovely to see was that with each

passing week the sermon got longer and it began to have some meat on it. I was very concerned that there was still no evidence of the Holy Spirit's involvement in this fellowship.

The leader's daughter was approaching her thirteenth birthday as I prayed about a gift for her, a very pretty booklet of scriptures I had bought on one occasion came to mind, however I was not sure if she would be allowed to read it as her Dad had very strict views on what he considered to be graven images. He would not allow her to have a children's illustrated bible as he considered the pictures to be against the ten commandments, in that they contained, he thought, graven images.

This booklet contained scriptures about the Holy Spirit! I was pretty sure that her Dad would read it first to make sure the book was suitable for his daughter, and he did! He became a changed man, he could not argue with the scriptures, and the more he read the more he depended on the Holy Spirit. His sermons became meat. I marveled at how the Lord through his Holy Spirit could cause such growth.

After three years he closed the church down as the numbers decreased, and his family stopped attending. It was time to move on!

But not before a friend and I had sought God

regarding using the Church building as a café - church. Something that was fast becoming a great source of outreach in our area. The building was ideally situated near the school, where lots of parents waited for their children. It had a down stairs entrance that was separate from the actual worship centre. Despite praying and talking to the owner we were not allowed to set up the café. Eventually the building was allowed to stand and rot, what a waste, all because of a lack of vision. While the leader believed in souls being saved he could only see that happening from the preaching of the word, not by friendship evangelism.

If you have never had this kind of relationship with your heavenly Father, I would encourage you to start immediately, seeking him because 'Now we can rejoice in our new relationship with God - all because of what our Lord Jesus has done for us in making us friends of God.'

Chapter Sixteen

When troubles assail us, God is still there behind the problems he is working it out. Psalm 34 states 'The Lord is close to the broken hearted and rescues those who are crushed in spirit.' We can learn much through suffering we could not learn any other way. We draw closer to him and he draws closer to us. We might ask how can we do this when we are hurting or suffering?

One of the issues I have struggled with in writing this book – is Autism. My family are riddled with it. My husband had it, his mother had it. Some of my children have it, many of my grandchildren have it. And now I have great grandchildren at least one of them has it! When will it end? When will this robbery of my family end?

Recently I was talking to one of my sons about how much I disclose of how much we as a family have suffered through this modern modern phenomenon. As

I write this I am still unsure how much I am going to reveal. In the press in Britain there has been much written about this curse as being down to bad parenting or lack of a fathers love in their lives, this is another finger that is pointed at families like mine. All these autistic people belong to Christian parents, that doesn't mean they have been perfect parents or imperfect for that matter.

The autistic gene is inherited and the experts believe this can cover more than one hundred different personality elements. Recently I watched a television programme made by Paddy McGuinnes a well-known television personality and his wife. They have three young children, all on the autistic spectrum. He was looking into what possible worthwhile future his children could have.

This has been in our thoughts as a family. What of the twenty-three-year-old who hasn't spoken since the day he had his triple vaccine at two years old. Where did the lively, vocal boy, a twin, disappear too? Could this really have been in his genes, lurking, waiting for such a moment to pounce and rob him of his life? Would he ever speak again? As I prayed I believed he would speak again. I blamed it on the vaccine, his father ------ my son, a nurse said no, it's genetic. Still I believe he will speak. Currently he is living independently in his own apartment, cared for by a carer who also looks after other young people with learning disabilities. He has a good life, he is happy, every photo I see of him he has a smile on his face and is jumping up and down or out walking through the countryside.

When he is in his own home he watches films in foreign languages, a sign surely that he speaks other languages in his head. That is now, but it hasn't always been so! In his youth he was very destructive, anything that belonged to his father he destroyed, punched holes in the doors. He could not discern what was edible, so everything harmful had to be locked away. Even food stuffs would be scattered across the floor. This took its toll on his parents' marriage and eventually after twenty-eight years, they divorced.

I have on rare occasions heard my grandson speak when I have been looking after him, just the odd word, like Granddad, as he looked out of the window and saw his Grandfather approaching.

Some kind people who worked with his Mother did some fund raising to send him to America to visit a centre that had, had some success with enabling autistic children to speak. I was living in Israel at the time and came back to look after the two other children while his parents took him to America. It was while he was being assessed that he told the assessors that he did not like going to his mother's family on a Sunday for lunch as they talked about him as though he could not understand what they were saying about him! How did they find that out? I don't know! That is why they are specialists in their field, and I'm not! His parents were told not to take him again, so my son stayed at home with him while his wife went with the other children each Sunday.

I was back in Israel the following Christmas when I received a phone call from son, wishing me a Happy Christmas. It nearly broke my heart, he was at home alone with his autistic son, while his wife went with the other children to her parents' home for Christmas dinner!

This young man is still full blown autistic at this time, but the Lord told me that when he is older he will speak and I don't believe God meant the sign language he uses at this present time.

Meanwhile his twin brother has also been affected by the autistic gene, he is only mildly affected, but struggled with his education. Currently he is at university studying theatre management. He has a beautiful singing voice and has performed on stage in many major musicals taking leading roles, now he is planning a career in the theatre.

I believe that the Lord has gifted both these young men and they will fulfill their potential. What of the other family members afflicted by this gene? My daughter who married a man with the same gene has three children with him, these all have some mild form of the disease, but are growing into beautiful young people, finding their way in life through the care and support of their loving mother. Sadly, as their father also has the gene, his influence is largely negative. Their eldest boy is now eighteen and he is showing signs of wanting to break his relationship with his father, he told me some time ago he could not accept God as Father as his experience of a father was not a good one.

For girls, one of the characteristic of this is problems can be issues with food, anorexia and bulimia are prevalent. This year my beautiful fourteen-year-old granddaughter nearly died due to this genetic disposition. Thankfully God saved her, but she requires a lot of support and watching by her mother. She is developing attitude and sass, gone is her lovely long hair replaced by a short cap of feathered hair which suits her tiny face. She is learning to play guitar and after many months off school is doing well in her schooling. She will make it, our warrior princess!

Finally, what of her Mother? I speak of her

provision as a much loved daughter in my previous book **'So you think you've messed up'**

Long before we knew anything about Autism and its effects on people and the lives of those associated with them I had given birth to two beautiful sons, but longed for a daughter I just did not feel complete. No matter how much I prayed I could not rid myself of the desire for a daughter. With the boys at school and fostering babies now my way of life, I continued to pray about a daughter, perhaps I would adopt one of the babies I fostered, went my thoughts. Then after almost seven years I became pregnant, the long awaited daughter was on the way! This beautiful baby was rejected at birth by her father, but I loved her, she was part of God's plan for me.

Now she is the mother of six children, clever talented children, the first two have university degrees, the third is autistic but is studying at college.

During these difficult times of Covid related lock downs, my daughter and I had not been able to meet up for a coffee, but finally we could! It was at this point in time more than forty-seven years after giving birth to my daughter she told me she had been diagnosed as being on the autistic spectrum. This had come about through our warrior princess being in hospital. Discussions with doctors about my granddaughter's condition had revealed that my daughter was autistic. She told me how she managed her life. A very busy mother and her work as a community worker. She masks it! What I wondered is masking it? She told me she has a face and manner that she wears at work and using this mask of the capable, friendly woman she is, gets her through her working day. When she gets home she puts on another mask, and plays another role! Being her mother is not covered by these masks, and to me she often presents an angry face! She told me that when she gets stressed with too much to do, she just can't put on another happy face, so I frequently get it. Now I know, I understand, I can cope with her off days. Practically I do what I can to help, that usually means picking some of the children up from school or looking after them when they were younger.

When I watched the recent television programme I mentioned earlier, Paddy Mc Guinness's wife discovered during the making of the programme that she too was autistic. Like my daughter she is on the clever end of the spectrum, his wife is now receiving help to overcome the difficulties she has faced as she became isolated in her own home, autistic people often find it difficult to make friends. Now she is beginning to make friends and push herself beyond her comfort zone. Watching this programme helped me to understand my daughter and her needs.

As a family we have gone from seeing my mother-in-law's strange way's in that she would never open any gift wrapped present you gave her. She would if you insisted, but she would pull the wrapping paper back and take a peep in but never took the gift out of its wrapping. When she died we found many years' worth of presents still in their wrappers, unopened and unused. To the displays of violence shown her by her son, who frequently when presented with food he did not want or disliked, would wipe the pots from the table with one blow, leaving the food and broken pots on the floor.

As I have studied and prayed through this genetic problem I am no clearer how to pray, nor any nearer to seeing them set free. There are so many different elements to it, all we can do is love and accept each person as they are. To quote a recent advert I saw 'Yes they are different, but love them anyway.' And I do.

Chapter Seventeen

Caleb, what do you know about him? Not a great deal probably because he is not mentioned very often in the Bible. He was one of two men who came back from the promised land and gave a good report of what the twelve men who had gone into the land to assess its potential had seen. Ten men said it was not worth looking at as it was full of giants. Two men, Caleb and Joshua said it was a great place and had brought the largest bunch of grapes anyone had ever seen to prove it! Still the children of Israel were not convinced and preferred to listen to the majority. He was forty years of age at that time.

Now aged eighty-five, he approaches Joshua the then leader of the tribe of Israel and asks for the land Moses had promised him all those years before. So Joshua blessed him and gave it to him, his promised land... Hebron. Despite his advancing years, Caleb felt as fit as he had when he was forty and went into that land and defeated the enemies.... The Anakites, those occupying the land and took it for himself.

I too received a promise from the Lord through the Holy Spirit. In my early years of prayer walking the streets of Jerusalem, the Holy Spirit directed my attention to a certain area of the city that I was not familiar with, it seemed as though this area was highlighted to me on the map of the city.

I spoke to Bob and Emily who ran the Christian guest house I was staying in, to enquire as to how to get to this particular area. They advised me not to go near that area as it was known to be very dangerous, many people having been robbed and murdered, it was not safe for a lone woman to visit the area. What should I do, I was only in Israel for another two days I needed to fulfil this task, I felt sure.

That evening I was talking to a lady I had become friendly with from South Korea. She said she would come with me, she thought it would be safer for two of us. We agreed to meet at a certain time in the following afternoon. When the agreed time came she didn't appear, I waited even though I knew she was leaving Israel that evening. Finally, I could wait no longer, I knew if I didn't leave then I would not complete my assignment. So with map in hand and my bottle of water I set off.

Suddenly I was moving like the cartoon character…. The road runner. My legs were moving like pistons. I reached the area I had seen highlighted on the map and I could feel the evil in the atmosphere, it was very heavy, but I pressed on and went through the spiritual darkness, I made it! When I reached the guest house, my Korean friend was there waiting for me. I told her I had completed the walk. She was amazed, because she said it should have taken me twice the length of time it seemed to have taken. She laughed when I told her how fast my legs had been moving.

On my flight home the Holy Spirit spoke to me. He said "Every place your foot has trod I will give you!" What did that mean, I have assumed that in eternity when the new heaven and earth are formed I will be allotted that area of Jerusalem as my inheritance, we shall see!

However, that has not been my only encounter with the Holy Spirit concerning Caleb.

Some years ago the Holy Spirit spoke to me through the scriptures, he said as Caleb had been, so would I. Coming into my promised land when like Caleb I reached the age of eighty-five. What does that mean? I haven't got a clue! Now almost eighty-two I am increasingly thinking on this promise, seeking the Lord and I know at the right time, if I am faithful, he will reveal the truth behind these words, and bring me into the promised land, whether here on earth or in heaven.

Jesus said "I no longer call you a servant, because a servant does not know his master's business. Instead I have called you friends, for everything that I learned from my Father I have made known to you."

It is through the Holy Spirit that he makes known to us his plans and purposes, we need to listen for that still small voice, learning to recognise it and remembering what he says. When he makes us a promise, he keeps it. He isn't a liar or changes his mind. The only reason we fail to come into his promises is that we fail to take on board what he is saying. We fail to hang on to those promises regardless of how impossible they may seem.

Chapter Eighteen

Let love be your aim

Which is the first commandment? It is 'Hear, O Israel, the Lord our God is one Lord. You shall love the Lord your God with all your heart, and with all your soul, with all your mind and with all your strength.' The second is 'You shall love your neighbour as yourself.'

God first, neighbour second, yourself last! Is that how it really is with us? As Christians our first love should be towards God, love for our partner or children or family should all follow on from there.

No matter what I say, what I believe, and what I do, I am bankrupt without love. Love means living the way God commanded us to live. How then are we to love? Gods answer? Love others as you love yourself.

Do you love yourself? I remember many years

ago thinking about this question, at that time I didn't love myself. Love had been in short supply in my family, I wasn't shown much love, so loving others was hard to do as I had no pattern to follow. However now as a Christian I did have someone to follow who demonstrated love. Jesus.

Jesus said "Truly I tell you, just as you did it to one of the least of these who are members of my family, you did it to me" We are to help and support our fellow believers, our brothers and sisters. As a young Christian I was greatly blessed by a group of women that I prayed with on a weekly basis, we were of different denominations, but all loved Jesus. As a family we were going through difficult financial times, my husband was only working part time as there was a national strike taking place.

I made the children's clothes by going to jumble sales and buying clothing that was made of good quality cloth and making it into something for the children to wear. These ladies often opened their purses and pour the contents into my lap, giving me the money I desperately needed to pay the household bills.

More recently during the Covid outbreak it has been my turn to open my purse and pour out its contents into some needy persons lap or give to some needy cause. I believe in our love for God we give the first fruits of our income to God in the form of a tithe. After that we give to others. Our love should not be just words and talk; it must be true love which shows itself in action.

So how do we love ourselves? In today's society being different is the key. Tattoo's make each person very unique, following fashion can make you stand out, body piercing, hair styles and colouring all give a person a unique look. While I don't doubt the Lord knew we would develop these differences, the love of ourselves does not stem from this kind of difference.

After all, if God loved us enough to send Jesus to die in our place, to take our sin upon himself, we should love ourselves. Sadly, we look at others and envy their looks, their gift's even their relationship with God and we want the same, we don't see ourselves as others see us. Kind, lovely, generous, caring for others. These are the things the Lord sees. Man looks at the outward appearance while the Lord looks at the heart.

We are to love ourselves as He has loved us.

A sense of shame can cause us to not like, let alone love ourselves. After my divorce I felt very ashamed, and yet I knew that God was in this. After much self-condemnation I realised the enemy of our souls was having a field day at my expense. I submitted myself to the Lord and told the enemy to clear off in Jesus name. He had to go!

When Adam and Eve sinned by being disobedient to God, they became ashamed and realised that they were naked and covered their bodies with leaves. When they confessed their sin to God, he covered them with animal skins for clothing, to cover their shame.

Likewise, when we have sinned and fallen from grace God in his mercy cleanses us from all sin as we confess our sin. We are covered by the blood of Jesus. Therefore, there is now no condemnation for those who are in Christ Jesus, who no longer walk in the flesh but by the Spirit. For the scriptures say that whoever believes in Him will not be put to shame. So if God loves us so much, we too should love ourselves.

We are bankrupt without love, and love is of the Holy Spirit.

If you would like more of the Holy Spirit in your life, just ask!

Dear Holy Spirit,

Come and fill me anew with your presence and power. If there is anything hindering me from receiving a fresh infilling of your power, please show me.

In Jesus name,

Amen.